Peasant Paintings
from Huhsien County

Compiled by
the Fine Arts Collection Section of
the Cultural Group Under the State Council of
the People's Republic of China

PEOPLE'S FINE ARTS PUBLISHING HOUSE

PEKING

Foreword

HUHSIEN COUNTY in China's Shensi Province is not only outstanding in learning from Tachai in agriculture but is also stepping out ahead in fine arts. The Great Proletarian Cultural Revolution and the deepening struggle of criticizing Lin Piao and Confucius, especially, have brought great changes to the area. With mounting enthusiasm and revolutionary drive the peasants of Huhsien County are wielding paintbrush and palette to occupy the ideological and cultural field in the countryside and have become masters of the socialist new culture. A group of poor and lower-middle peasant artists, painting as a spare-time activity, adhere to the orientation pointed out in Chairman Mao's "Talks at the Yenan Forum on Literature and Art" and are training and maturing in the storm of two-line and class struggle. They are continuing with firm steps their march forward along Chairman Mao's revolutionary line in literature and art.

The works of these peasant painters are militant and have broad mass appeal. All the artists are people's commune members — women, youngsters and old people, Party secretaries, production team leaders, militia company commanders and accountants. They are all pathbreakers in production and at the same time an advance force in culture. With hoe in one hand and brush in the other and taking the Party's basic line as their guide to action, they are active in the three great revolutionary movements of class struggle, the struggle for production and scientific experiment and in carrying out the central task at each step of the revolution. They have produced tens of thousands of paintings reflecting these struggles, warmly acclaiming Chairman Mao's proletarian revolutionary line, the socialist new countryside and the resounding victory of the Great Proletarian Cultural Revolution, while condemning revisionism and the bourgeoisie. They use revolutionary art **"for uniting and educating the people and for attacking and destroying the enemy"** and have helped to develop the socialist economic base and consolidate the proletarian dictatorship.

The Huhsien County peasant artists persist in painting on a spare-time basis so as never to be separated from the three great revolutionary struggles. They have correctly handled the relationship between politics and art and between the superstructure and the economic base and put into practice the principle of art serving the workers, peasants and soldiers, serving socialism and proletarian politics. They have set a pattern for developing fine arts as a spare-time activity in rural areas and become a model for professional artists.

The broad masses of poor and lower-middle peasants grasping the artist's brush and wielding power in the cultural as well as in the political field is a deep-going revolution in the superstructure. It shows that the working people are not only the creators of man's social material wealth but are also the creators of man's intellectual wealth, that the working people are indeed the masters of history. This fact powerfully refutes the reactionary fallacies of Lin Piao and Confucius who trumpeted the idealist theory of "innate genius" and "the highest are the wise and the lowest are the stupid." It is also an antidote to the symptoms and influence of the revisionist line in contemporary art.

The album presents a selection from paintings exhibited in Peking in 1973 with the addition of several more recent works.

The compilers

May 1974

Contents

Huhsien County's New Look. *Tung Cheng-yi*

Listening to the Good News. *Liu Chih-kuei*

Reading the Tenth Party
Congress Communique.
Chang Hsing-lung

The Whole Family Studies the Communique.   *Tu Chih-lien*

A Painting in the Class-Education Exhibition, Niutung People's Commune (No. 1).

There's a fine situation of upsurge,   In the forward march 'mid battle songs,
Refuting Lin and correcting work styles.   The East wind stirs red flags for thousands of miles.

Niutung People's Commune Spare-Time Art Group

A Painting in the Class-Education Exhibition, Niutung People's Commune (No. 2).

One rafter does not make a house,   Organized, we have strength,
Nor a single brick a wall;   And wide is the great bright road.

Niutung People's Commune Spare-Time Art Group

A Painting in the Class-Education Exhibition, Niutung People's Commune (No. 3).

Chairman Mao points out the bright road,
The people are happy now the commune's set up;
Uproot the ages-long stark poverty,
Plant seeds of prosperity for generations to come.

Niutung People's Commune Spare-Time Art Group

A Painting in the Class-Education Exhibition, Niutung People's Commune (No. 4).

Dancing are the Chinling Mountains,
Laughing the Weishui River.
The revolutionary committee's been set up,

Revisionism's on the run; our
Rivers and mountains will be red forever.

Niutung People's Commune Spare-Time Art Group

A Painting in the Class-Education Exhibition, Niutung People's Commune (No. 5).

Yenan's sons and daughters, with firm fighting will,
Dare to give the land a new look;

They work hard and fast to gain a rich harvest;
Tachai flowers' perfume spreads everywhere.

Niutung People's Commune Spare-Time Art Group

Condemning Confucius at His Temple Gate.   *Chao Kun-han*

Exhibition Repudiating
Lin Piao and Confucius.
Yang Chih-hsien

Grasp the Gun Firmly. *Sung Hou-cheng*

Criticizing Lin Piao and Confucius Promotes Production.
Hang Kao-she

Old Party Secretary.
Liu Chih-teh

Party Class.   *Liu Chih-kuei*

Grasp Revolution, Promote Production.
Liu Hui-sheng

Night Battle. *Kao Chih-min*

Today's "Foolish Old Men" Create New Scenes (Scrolls 1 and 2). *Cheng Min-sheng and Chang Lin*

Today's "Foolish Old Men" Create New Scenes (Scrolls 3 and 4). *Cheng Min-sheng and Chang Lin*

The Tempo of
Tamping.
Wang Yung-yi

Digging a Well. *Fan Chih-hua*

Well-Digging on
a Snowy Night.
Li Keh-min

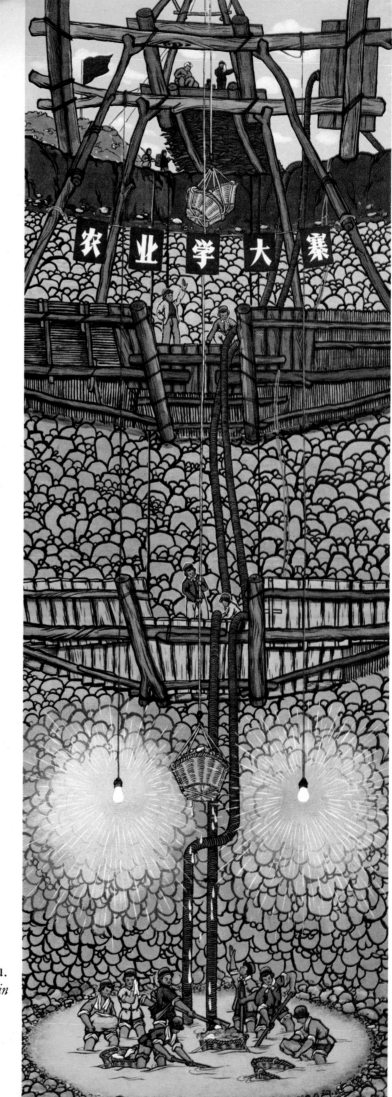

Digging a Well on the Plateau.
Li Keh-min

Wintertime Warmth. *Chang Hsing-lung*

Spring Hoeing. *Li Feng-lan*

Preparing for Cotton Planting. *Li Shun-hsiao*

**Before the
Summer Harvest.**
*Niutung People's Commune
Spare-Time Art Group*

Brigade Repair Shop. *Wu Shui-lung*

Prefabricated Parts
for the Worksite.
Chia Keh-chiang

The Motor's Roar. *Li Keh-min*

Brigade Pumping Station. *Wu Sheng-chin*

Buying "Iron Oxen."   *Hsieh Chang-chang*

Sprinkling.
Yang Yang-tung

Fertilizing the Cotton Field. *Chang Fang-hsia*

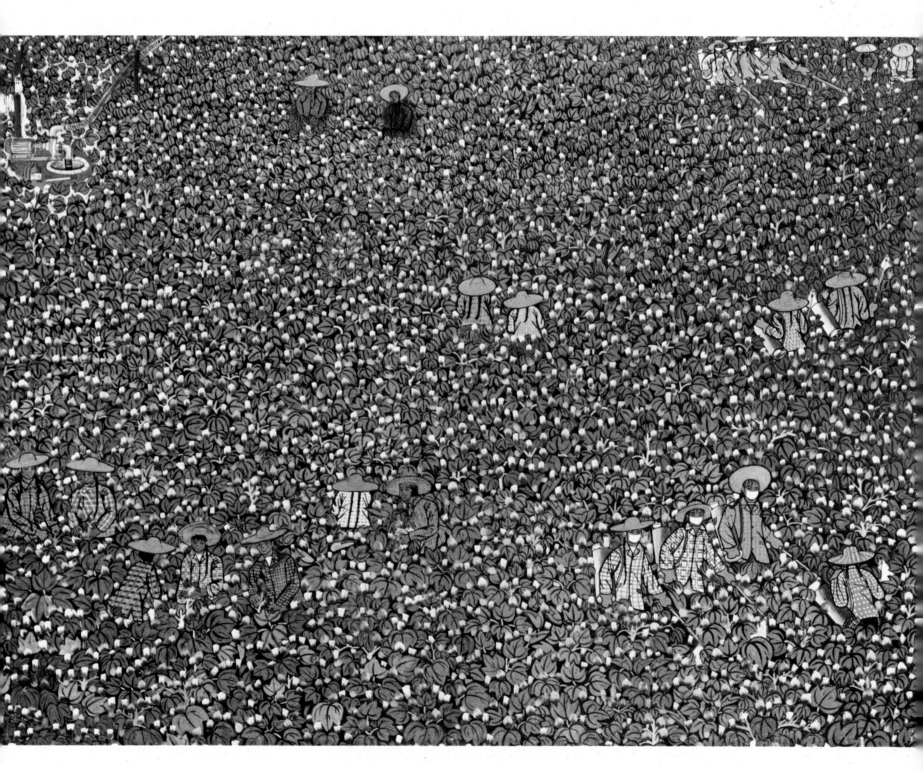

Cultivating Cotton. *Hsu Heng-ko*

Wresting the Harvest.   *Ko Cheng-min*

Women Hold Up
Half the Sky.
Cheng Min-sheng

The Twelfth Good
Harvest Year.
Pai Hsu-hao

Scene of Bumper Harvest.   *Yang Chih-hsien*

Scientific Farming Gets Results. *Liu Fang*

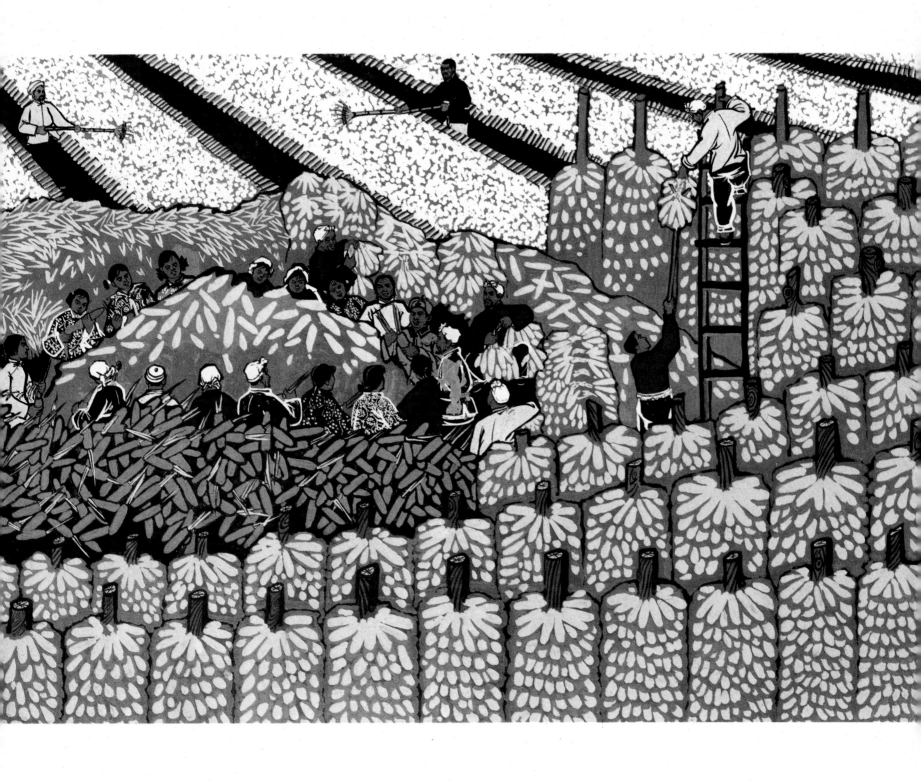

Golden Hills, Silver Sea. *Li Shun-hsiao*

Happy Harvest of Cotton. *Li Feng-lan*

Fruit, Large and Juicy. *Wu Sheng-chin*

Sunning Wheat. *Li Chen-hua*

Drying New Cotton. *Ma Ya-li*

"Storing Grain Everywhere." *Ma Ya-li*

Cotton Purchasing Station.
Liu Hui-sheng

Delivering Grain to the State. *Chou Wen-teh*

Grain for the State. *Ko Cheng-min*

Brigade Pig Farm.
Liu Hsu-hsu

On-the-Spot Meeting. *Ma Chien-ya*

Never Stop Being Industrious and Thrifty. *Chang Lin*

Commune
Persimmon Grove.
Wen Chih-chiang

Cultivating Medicinal Herbs.   *Pai Hsu-hao*

54

Flourishing Side-Line Occupations. *Pai Tien-hsueh*

Gathering the Commune's Lotus-Root.   *Tu Chien-jung*

Commune Fish Pond. *Tung Cheng-yi*

Brigade Chicken Farm. *Ma Ya-li*

Brigade Ducks. *Li Chen-hua*

Pepper Harvest. *Su Chun-liang*

Cabbage. *Chiao Tsai-yun*

Raising Silkworms. *Wu Sheng-chin*

Spare-Time Practice Shooting. *Chang Chun-hsia*

Night Watch.   *Shen Chen-tung and Yang Chih-hsien*

Rural Supply and Marketing Co-operative. *Ko Cheng-min*

Every Family Has a Bank Account. *Liu Hui-sheng*

Brigade Tailor Shop. *Chang Chun-hsia*

Learning to Sing Revolutionary Model Operas. *Pai Tien-hsueh*

The Library Comes to the Fields.   *Yang Shui-teh and Hsin Chiang-lung*

Basketball Match in a Mountain Village.   *Pai Tien-hsueh*

No End of Bumper
Harvest Pictures.
Chao Kun-han

Revolutionary Culture Takes Hold in the Countryside.
Chang Lin

Rural Health Station.
Liu Chih-teh

Brigade Clinic.
Li Cheng-hsuan

Exchanging Horse-Raising Experience. *Yen Kuang-hui*

Spring in the
Chinling Mountains.
*Chintu People's Commune
Spare-Time Art Group*

Cotton Fields in
the Mountains.
Wang Fu-lai

On the Banks of
the Laoho River.
Cheng Min-sheng

New Look of a Village.
Niutung People's Commune Spare-Time Art Group

New Mountain Scene.
Chao Chun-min

户县农民画选集

中华人民共和国国务院文化组

美术作品征集小组编

*

人民美术出版社出版（北京）

1976年（8开）第一版

编号：8027·5871

84—E—365

P